Mary Amanda

Carcinoma on the floor of the pelvis

Mary Amanda

Carcinoma on the floor of the pelvis

ISBN/EAN: 9783337873691

Printed in Europe, USA, Canada, Australia, Japan

Cover: Foto ©ninafisch / pixelio.de

More available books at **www.hansebooks.com**

CARCINOMA

ON THE

FLOOR OF THE PELVIS

BY

MARY A. DIXON JONES, M.D.

BROOKLYN, N. Y.

Reprinted from the MEDICAL RECORD, March 11, 1893

NEW YORK
TROW DIRECTORY, PRINTING AND BOOKBINDING CO.
201-213 EAST TWELFTH STREET
1893

CARCINOMA ON THE FLOOR OF THE PELVIS.

THE patient was near fifty years of age, and apparently in excellent health. She had been treated for many years by various physicians for displacement of the uterus and other pelvic miseries which are supposed to result therefrom, but without relief. She said she was growing steadily worse, and that at times her sufferings were most intense.

I found the uterus drawn to the extreme right, and, with the corresponding tube and ovary, fixed by inflammatory adhesions. The left uterine appendages were prolapsed and adherent to a mass, the size of a small orange, in the centre of the pelvic floor. This mass or tumor was soft, extremely sensitive, and with some apparent fluctuation. Her last physician, diagnosing it to be a misplaced uterus, had from time to time made various and continued efforts to put the supposed organ in position. These manipulations gave the patient great distress, the pain often lasting several days. I advised the immediate removal of the tumor as her only chance of recovery. Her husband was anxious that the operation should be performed, but wished it to be done in his own home, and requested me to call and make the necessary arrangements. I refused to perform such an operation unless every circumstance, as far as I could judge, was the most favorable for the patient's recovery. I recommended certain changes in a portion of their beautiful home, but, as the simplicity and asepsis of a hospital can rarely be established in a private residence, I suggested that the patient enter the hospital. Doctor E. A. Wheeler, who had advised the patient to consult me, also thought it best. She entered the Woman's Hospital, of Brooklyn, on March 16, 1888. So much had she suffered that she said to me the day before the operation, "If you were to tell me that I had but one chance in twenty-five, I would take that chance and have the operation."

The operation was performed on March 19, 1888. I removed first the left tube and ovary, with the tumor to which they were adherent. All had grown so firmly to the floor of the pelvis that the separation was attended with great difficulty, and followed by severe hemorrhage, which was almost uncontrollable. Nothing checked it but securely clamping the torn edges of the wound, and for this I used forceps whose handles projected beyond the abdominal incision. I had previously removed considerable portion of what I supposed to be affected tissue. The pseudo-membranous adhesions which bound the uterus and right uterine appendages were separated and the latter removed. The peritoneal cavity was thoroughly flushed with water sterilized by heat; a drainage-tube was introduced, and for still more thorough drainage a large strip of gauze was inserted in the abdominal wound, extending beneath the line of sutures down to the floor of the pelvis. The abdominal wound was dressed, the patient placed comfortably in bed, and, in every respect, she seemed to be doing well. Still there were indications that the disease was malignant, and I had little hope of her recovery. Statistics show that operations for malignant disease of the abdomen are almost invariably fatal.[1]

The patient came comfortably out of ether. In two

[1] In 1881, in St. Luke's Hospital, 2 cases of malignant tumor of the abdomen, 2 deaths. In New York State Woman's Hospital, in 1885, 2 cases of carcinoma of omentum, exploratory incision, death; carcinoma of ovary, ovariotomy, death In 1886, 3 carcinomata of omentum, exploratory incision, all died; sarcoma, exploratory incision, death. In 1887, 2 cases of carcinomata of omentum, both died of shock after exploratory incision; carcinoma ovarii, ovariotomy, death; sarcoma ovarii, ovariotomy, death. In 1886, cancer of ovaries, exploratory incision, death.

hours the drainage-tube was drawn off, the dressings were found fully saturated with bloody serum, and new dressings were applied. So for several days three or four times in the twenty-four hours the wound was redressed, and in twenty hours the forceps and gauze were removed. I believe that the packing of the peritoneal cavity with the gauze saved the patient's life. She continued to improve, and in five weeks was able to leave the hospital. She did so well that I dismissed the idea of the disease being malignant, and it was not until the eighth day of the following December, nine months after the operation, when, in due course, I studied microscopically the specimen, and found that it was a cancer, and portions of it were of a most malignant type. The left tube and ovary were both found infiltrated with cancerous growth. The right tube also showed inflammatory reaction, and gave indications that the cancer was rapidly spreading.

The same day I discovered this condition, I sent for the husband and Dr. Wheeler. I informed the former of his wife's condition, and that in the natural course of the disease the patient could not live more than a few months. Dr. Wheeler said, and as he afterward wrote me, "There was no doubt the operation had greatly prolonged the patient's life, and relieved in a great measure her sufferings;" still it was evident the malignant degeneration had been existing only about one year, and if the growth had been removed at an earlier period, or before it had infiltrated surrounding structures, the disease might have been entirely eradicated and the patient saved.

Cancer is primarily a local disease induced by local irritation. Dr. George F. Shrady, in his invaluable article on "The Curability of Cancer by Operation," says: "The disease has a local origin, and is, therefore, removable, and the constitution becomes affected only secondarily by a more or less dissemination of original cancer-germs."[1]

In this instance the disease was clearly of local origin.

[1] MEDICAL RECORD, January, 1887.

The patient had been sick since the birth of her last child, then thirteen years of age. At that time there was some sepsis, which resulted in pelvic peritonitis, salpingitis, and oöphoritis, followed by the displacement of the Fallopian tubes and ovaries, and the formation of pseudo-membranous adhesions. Repeated attacks of peritonitis increased the disease, and the long-continued local irritation developed the cancer, which finally ended her existence.[1]

If the uterine appendages in this patient had been removed eight or ten years previously, the source of the irritation would have been removed, and the development of cancer in all probability prevented. At that time, too, the necessary surgical interference would have been comparatively simple. Still, if the operation had then been performed, we would doubtless have been told of " mutilating and preventing women from having children." Yet we notice in all these thirteen years this woman had no child, the disease that had caused the suffering had produced an incurable sterility, and rendered her life one continued period of invalidism. In almost every instance perhaps, without exception, when this operation is needed, a woman is, by her very condition, already rendered sterile; and it is as good surgery to remove such diseased organs as to amputate a limb for the various causes considered necessary.

The case of this pelvic tumor has been one of exceeding interest to me, and from time to time I have returned to the study of it; but repeated and careful microscopical examinations have not only left unsettled the question as to the cause of the disease, but even as to where the cancer started. According to modern views, first announced by Thiersch and Waldeyer, a normal epithelial structure is required for giving rise to cancer. There is no such structure on the floor of the pelvis, unless we resort to the hypothesis that a parovary was the initial source of the growth of the cancer, which I cannot prove. A sufficient

[1] She died thirteen months after the operation, a large secondary growth in the peritoneal cavity.

number of cases is, however, on record, where cancer has started in pure connective-tissue formations, entirely devoid of epithelial structure, such as the medulla of the bone, the pleura, the peritoneum, or lymph ganglia; and cancer has occasionally been found in the substances of the brain, independent of the epithelia of the ventricles. Cohnheim's hypothesis that embryonal epithelial germs may have been spread in the connective tissue and caused the appearance of the cancer, is unfounded, it tries to explain one puzzle by another, and has been justly discarded by pathologists.

The humoral pathologists have held that cancer is an outcome of a constitutional disturbance, more especially a faulty state of the blood. This cannot be, because we find that almost uniformly only persons of good constitution will have cancer, more especially in advanced years, or after the thirtieth year of life. This patient had naturally a strong constitution, her father is now living at the age of eighty-nine years.

The tumor, with the adjacent organs and tubes, was placed in a dilute solution of chromic acid until thoroughly hardened, and afterward sliced for the microscopical research. The main tumor exhibits three varieties of cancer, *i.e.*, scirrhous, adenoid, and medullary cancer. See Fig. 1.

The scirrhous portion appeared to be composed of an extremely dense and firm fibrous connective tissue, with scanty nests of epithelia dispersed in it. The connective tissue is made up of coarse bundles distinctly interlacing, so much so that longitudinal sections of the bundles alternate with cross and oblique sections. It is mainly in the cross-sections that we meet with epithelial nests. In many places the protoplasmic bodies between the bundles, the so-called connective-tissue cells, are enlarged, or found in a state of active proliferation by a more or less pronounced outgrowth of living matter. In such places the splitting up of the protoplasmic bodies into rows and chains of nucleated, coarsely granular bodies, is plainly seen. Even

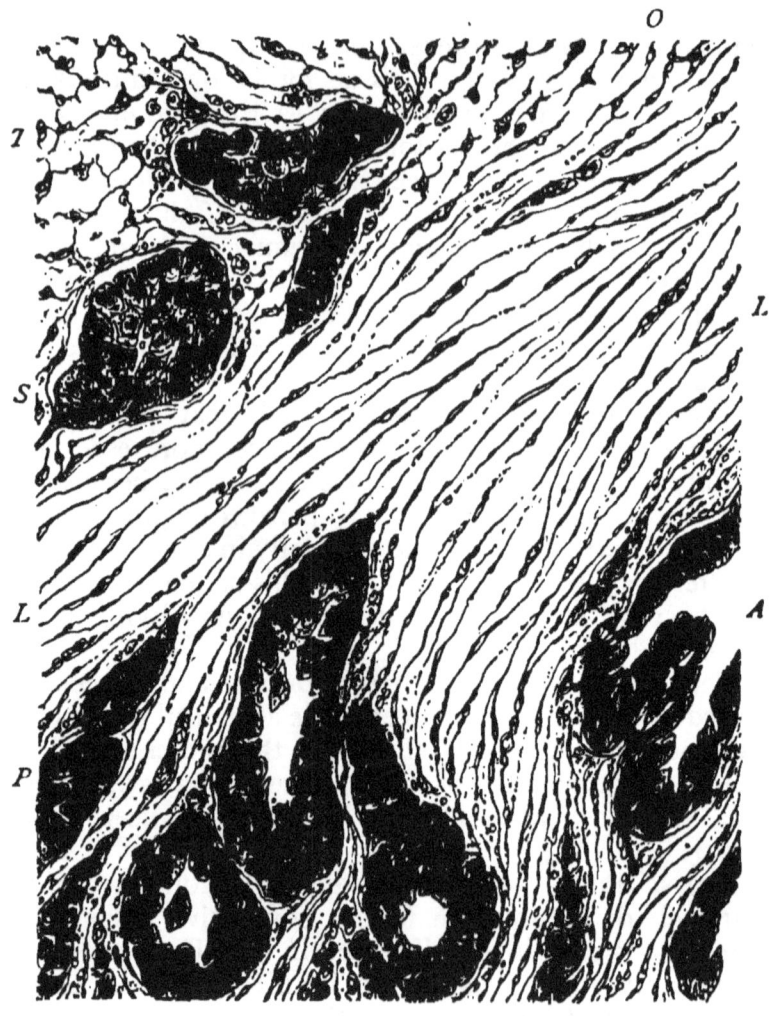

FIG. 1.—Carcinoma of Floor of Pelvis, Scirrhous and Adenoid Portion. × 200. *L, L*, longitudinal bundles of coarse fibrous connective tissue ; *O*, oblique bundles ; *T*, transverse bundles of coarse fibrous connective tissue ; *S*, small nests of cancer epithelia, the scirrhous portion ; *A*, gland-like formations of cancer epithelia, the adenoid portion.

in the scirrhous portion we not unfrequently meet with nests hollowed out in their centre, thereby showing a tendency to change into the adenoid variety. The epithelia of the nests are small, provided with distinct nuclei and nucleoli, and separated from one another by a light rim of cement substance traversed by delicate thread-like formations.

Close by we meet with the variety termed "adenoid," or gland-like. This form is conspicuous by epithelial nests hollowed out in their centre into more or less regular cavities typical of all glandular tissue. At the same time we notice a change in the form of the epithelia, which have become columnar, being attached with narrow feet to the surrounding layer of connective tissue, whereas their bases project toward the central calibre. In this way tubular formations are produced with manifold convolutions of the subjacent connective tissue as well as the lining epithelium. With high powers we can ascertain that many epithelia are enlarged and contain globular and irregular secondary formations in their interior which have been considered by pathologists as parasitic in nature. I hold the view of Virchow, that all these impacted formations are signs of active proliferation of the epithelia, the so-called "mother-cells," of old authors, tending toward a new formation of epithelia. The adenoid form of cancer is most frequently met with in the uterus and in the alimentary tract, although in this case I was unable to trace any connection of the cancerous tumor with either the uterus or the rectum.

The third variety of cancer observed in this tumor is the so-called medullary form, which pathologists justly consider the most malignant. See Fig. 2.

We see some scanty tubular formations of adenoid cancer blending with a portion characterized by an abundance of epithelial nests and comparatively little fibrous connective tissue between them. Both the scirrhous and adenoid forms have contributed to produce the medullary type. The nests, though peg-like in the vicinity of the tubules, have assumed rather irregular forms, in which even the single epithelia have, in many instances, lost their angular shape to such a degree that a large protoplasmic layer may appear with scattered nuclei and occasional demonstrations of single epithelia, which, however, under all circumstances, remain interconnected by means of delicate threads.

In the adjacent connective tissue we see an active proliferation, most pronounced in the medullary portion of

FIG. 2.—Carcinoma of Floor of Pelvis, Adenoid and Medullary Portion × 200. *A*, adenoid or gland-like formations of cancer-epithelia ; *M*, *M*, medullary portion of cancer ; *I*, *I*, so-called small cellular or inflammatory infiltration of fibrous connective tissue ; *F*, longitudinal bundles of coarse fibrous connective tissue ; *N*, beginning formations of nests between the bundles.

the tumor. There are numerous granules and globules scattered throughout the connective tissue. This infiltration has long since been known by the name of "small cellular infiltration of Virchow," or "inflammatory reaction" of Thiersch and Waldeyer. It is interesting to inquire what may be the origin and significance of this proliferation in the connective tissue adjacent to all cancer nests, more especially to the adenoid and medullary varieties. The image offered by the connective tissue closely resembles the inflammatory condition. See Fig. 3.

We know that every new-growth in the connective tissue first appears as a reduction to its medullary or embryonal condition, the same as takes place in ordinary inflammation. Both cancer and sarcoma, in their commencement, present appearances similar to inflammation. It is only the final result that will determine the nature of the exuberant growth of the connective tissue or the epithelium, whether it is simply an acute inflammatory disturbance or a malignant tumor, sarcoma, or carcinoma.

Around every growth we see this inflammatory reaction or infiltration. Virchow says: "If we examine any proliferating tumor of a cellular character, we find, three to five lines beyond its apparent limits, the tissue already in a state of disease and exhibiting the first traces of a new zone." [1]

When studying with high powers of the microscope this "inflammatory infiltration," I noticed that some of the inflammatory corpuscles were shaping themselves into cancer epithelia; the indifferent or medullary corpuscles were changing to large polyhedral epithelia, and forming cancer nests. This, so far as I know, had never before been observed or demonstrated, and it completely sustains what Dr. C. Heitzman asserted in 1883, that the so-called "small cellular infiltration" of the connective tissue was the "pre-stage of cancer." [2]

[1] Cellular Pathology, p. 503.
[2] Microscopical Morphology.

This view is of great practical importance. Whenever we see by the microscope this infiltration on the cut surface made by the surgeon, we can positively foretell a recurrence of the cancer in the given spot. We will always

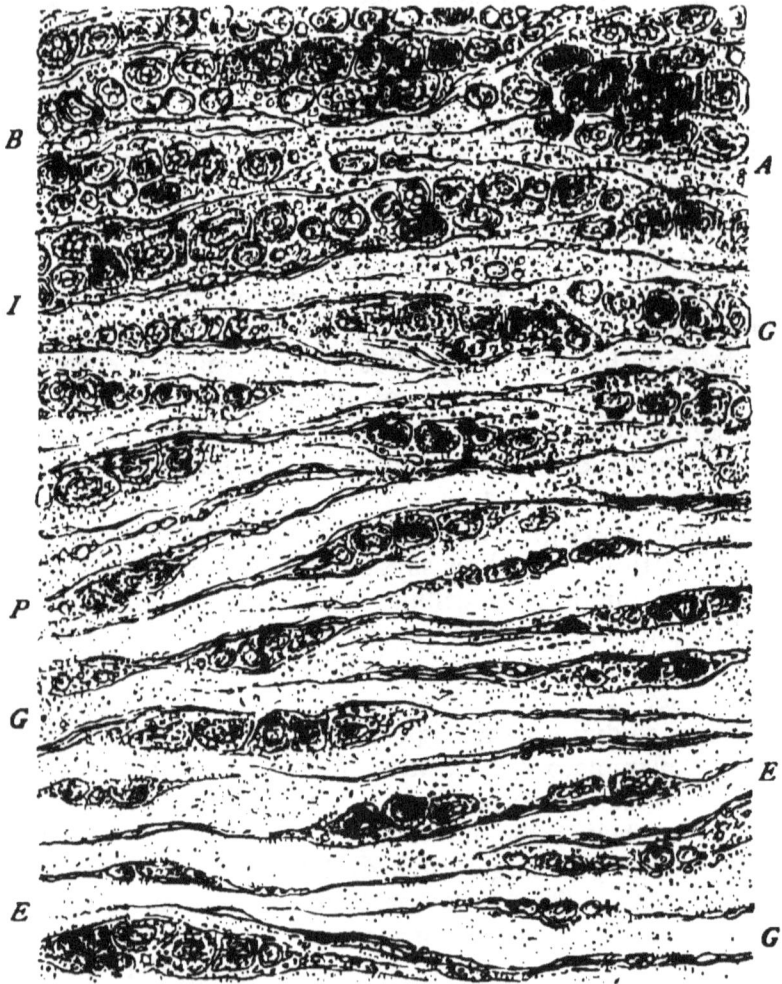

FIG. 3.—So-called Small Cellular or Inflammatory Infiltration of Fibrous Connective Tissue Near Cancer. × 600. *I, I*, Interstices between the bundles, enlarged, holding lumps of living matter; *B, B*, basis substance of bundles unchanged; *P*, Transformation of basis substance into protoplasm; *G, G*, globular bodies sprung both from the interstitial protoplasm and the bundles; *E, E*, angular cancer-epithelia, the products of globular bodies.

find "this zone is the chief source of local recurrences after extirpation."[1] In 1884, Dr. Paul Mundé[2] reported that after removing a uterus he gave it to Dr. C. Heitzman for microscopical examination; the latter noticed on a vestige of the vaginal wall this infiltration, and said, in his report: "Should my view be correct that this infiltration is a preliminary stage of cancer, no doubt recurrence will take place in your case within two years." The disease recurred in seven months. Virchow strictly holds to the view that in the fibrous connective tissue nothing else is capable of proliferation but the so-called cells. Since 1873 it has been shown that the fibrous basis substance has the same structure as protoplasm, and the living portion of this, arranged in the shape of a reticulum, is capable of proliferation just the same as the protoplasm itself.

This view necessarily upset all the assertions of the cellular pathologists to the effect that only cells proper are capable of proliferation. In 1880, S. Stricker, in Vienna, accepted these views, and quite recently P. Grawitz, of Griefswald, Germany, has corroborated them and has shown that the basis substance in morbid conditions may be transformed into protoplasmic bodies, for which he suggests the rather awkward title, "slumbering cells." He imagines that every fibre of the connective tissue is a cell, dormant as it were, until brought forth to light by an irritative process, either inflammatory or from the growth of a tumor.

Fig. 3 plainly shows the transformation of the basis substances into protoplasm. Both the free protoplasm between the bundles and the protoplasm of the basis substance grow and proliferate. We see rows of newly formed elements between the bundles, and the bundles themselves transformed into protoplasmic bodies, the final result being what pathologists term "inflammatory infiltration."

In the highest degree of this change only scanty spindle-

[1] Cellular Pathology. [2] Gynecological Transactions, 1884.

shaped fibrilla are left between the groups of the embryonal or medullary corpuscles. At the same time we see that in the groups of medullary corpuscles numerous bodies had made their appearance characterized by an angular shape, by mutual flattening, and the appearance of large oblong nuclei; in short, bodies which offer all evidences of epithelia, although they had made their appearance, independently of previous cancer nests, in the midst of embryonal or medullary corpuscles sprung from previous fibrous connective tissue. This observation corroborates the view, first announced by Virchow, that cancer epithelia may originate from the cells of fibrous connective tissue, and also from the basis substance.

The microscopical analysis of both ovaries revealed still more remarkable facts serving to illustrate the manner in which cancer is spreading. The right ovary was found in the state of the reactive infiltration just described. This may have been the result of a mere oöphoritis, or of a beginning appearance of cancer. Since the right ovary contained several gyromata, and the inflammatory infiltration was most pronounced in the cortex of the ovary, and in the vicinity of the gyromata, I would consider part of this, at least, as subacute oöphoritis. Quite different were the features in the left ovary. See Fig. 4.

Here we see already with low powers of the microscope peculiar tracts pervading the medullary portion near the hilum. These tracts show coarsely granular, irregular bodies clustered together in the shape of rows, exhibiting all the features of cancer nests. Higher powers of the microscope reveal the interesting facts that these rows of cancer nests are in the lymph-vessels, and that the lymph-vessels are dilated by, and are carrying the cancer epithelia. This proves, what has long been surmised, that cancer is conveyed to different and distant parts of the body by means of the lymphatics; but this is, so far as I know, the first time it has been seen, or the fact positively verified, though it has generally been supposed to be the case, because the lymph ganglia near a malignant growth are the

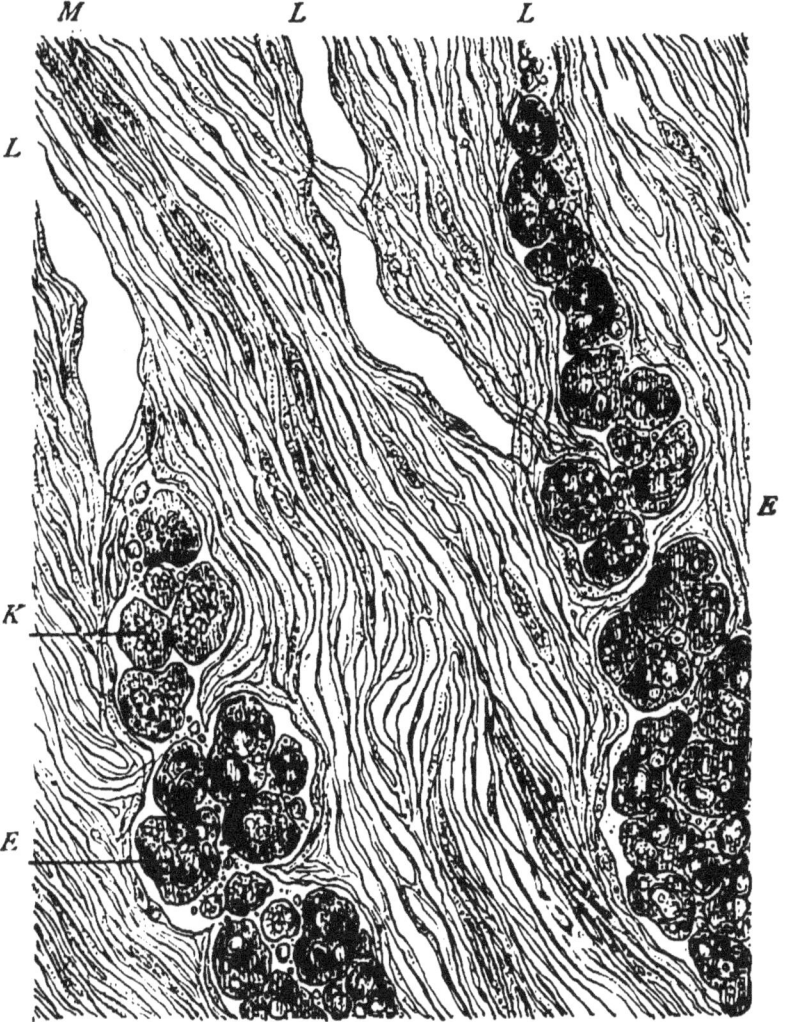

FIG. 4.—Thrombosis of Lymph-vessels of Left Ovary with Cancer Epithelia. × 600. *C*, fibrous connective tissue of medulla of ovary near hilum ; *M*, bundles of smooth muscle fibres ; *L, L, L*, lymph-vessels with unchanged endothelial lining ; *E, E*, cancer epithelia filling and extending the calibres of lymph-vessels ; *K*, cancer epithelia whose nuclei show karyokinetic figures.

first to be affected. The endothelial lining of lymph-vessels are most conspicuous in the dilated portions, where the cancer epithelia did not entirely fill the calibre. In the lymph-vessels the cancer epithelia have mostly lost their angular shape, being more or less rounded and coarsely granular, and showing a considerable increase of living matter toward an endogenous new formation. Some epithelia (K) show a karyokinetic change of the nuclei which leads to a division of the cancer epithelia. Besides these formations we meet with protoplasmic bodies mixed with epithelia not surpassing in size so-called lymph corpuscle, and between all these formations granules of varying sizes.

In Fig. 4 an entirely recent thrombus of the lymphatics is illustrated, which is proved by the fact that as yet no change has taken place in the walls of the lymphatics or in their endothelia. That such changes do occur, and give rise to secondary tissue-changes in the vicinity of the lymphatics, is proven by the study of other portions of the same specimen. See Fig. 5.

Here we notice peculiar changes of cancer epithelia, not only the indistinct karyokinetic change in some nuclei, but also a direct division of the epithelia into smaller pieces of protoplasm, known by the name of medullary or embryonal corpuscles. Whether the division is an indirect or direct one, the result is the same under all circumstances; it is the living matter of the protoplasm or the epithelia stored up in the nuclei and the granules in the surrounding protoplasm that causes proliferation.

Along the border of the lymph-vessels we still recognize the endothelia, which likewise are in a beginning proliferation by the outgrowth of their living matter into, first, coarsely granular, afterward vacuolated, and at last nucleated and reticulated bodies, exactly as we see in an acute inflammatory process. In several places in the specimen the wall of the lymph-vessel is completely lost by inflammatory changes of the adjacent fibrous connective tissue. Both the connective-tissue corpuscles and the basis substance have undergone proliferation, which may lead to the appearance of medullary or inflammatory corpuscles, changes which penetrate the environments of

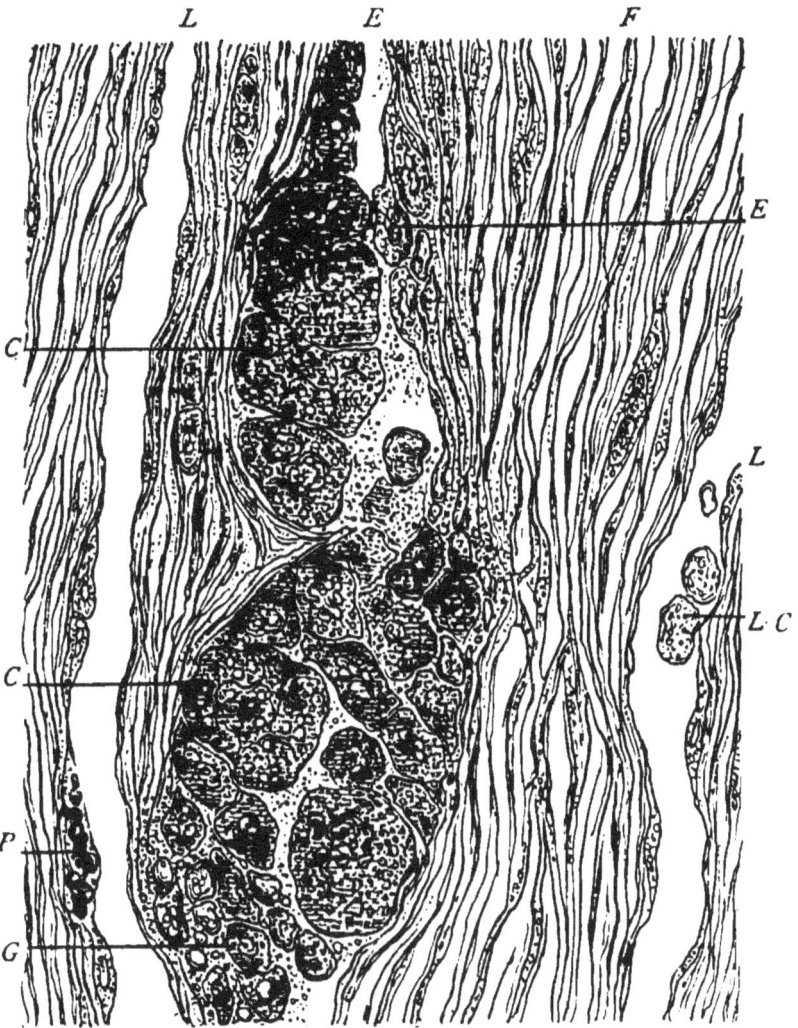

FIG. 5.—Cancerous Invasion of Connective Tissue from Cancer Epithelia Transported into Lymph-Vessels. × 600. *F*, fibrous connective tissue ; *L*, *L*, lymph-vessels ; *L*, *C*, lymph-corpuscles ; *P*, pigment cluster from previous hemorrhage ; *C*, *C*, cancer epithelia lying in lymph-vessels ; *E*, *E*, endothelia of lymph-vessel in proliferation ; *G*, outgrowth of living matter in endothelia and adjacent connective tissue.

the lymph-vessels to a varying depth, and as stated before, to be considered the commencement or pre-stage of a cancerous growth. One of the endothelia of an apparently normal lymph-vessel is illustrated at *L, C*. It shows a cluster of red-brown pigment granules, due to a previous hemorrhage. In what relation this hemorrhage may have been to the cancerous growth, I am unable to say.

¶ It will be understood that the thrombosis of cancer epithelia is only in real lymph-vessels lined by endothelia, and never in the so-called juice-canals, which by Recklinghausen and his followers have been considered as the roots of the lymph-vessels, destitute of a wall proper. All researches since 1874 have proven the fallacy of this view, since the juice-canals are nothing but spaces filled with protoplasm and by no means in an open communication with lymph-vessels proper. Unquestionably we do succeed in driving colored liquids into the spaces filled with protoplasm, surrounded by a basis substance of more or less considerable resistance. By this procedure the protoplasm is compressed and pushed to the wall of the cavity, where we invariably find its vestiges. Neither has the silver method proven the existence of juice-canals, since the apparently empty spaces have always been shown to be filled with protoplasm by the stain with chloride of gold.

The highest powers of the microscope thoroughly convince the observer of the tissue changes occurring around a cancerous thrombus in a lymph-canal. See Fig. 6.

The illustrated spot is more advanced in such changes than those drawn in Fig. 5. We see some nuclei in karyokinetic changes. In many epithelia the nuclei are broken up into a number of irregular lumps of living matter. We see a division of some epithelia into smaller pieces of protoplasm, interconnected with some original epithelia by delicate threads. The lining endothelia of the distended lymph-vessels are changed everywhere, the changes consisting in an increase of the living matter of both the nucleus and the granules of the protoplasm. At the same time the adjacent connective tissue exhibits beautiful figures of proliferation from a small, just perceptible, granule into a solid, later a vacuoled, and at last nucleated mass of living matter, the last form being that usually described by the authors "protoplasm" or "cells." The basis sub-

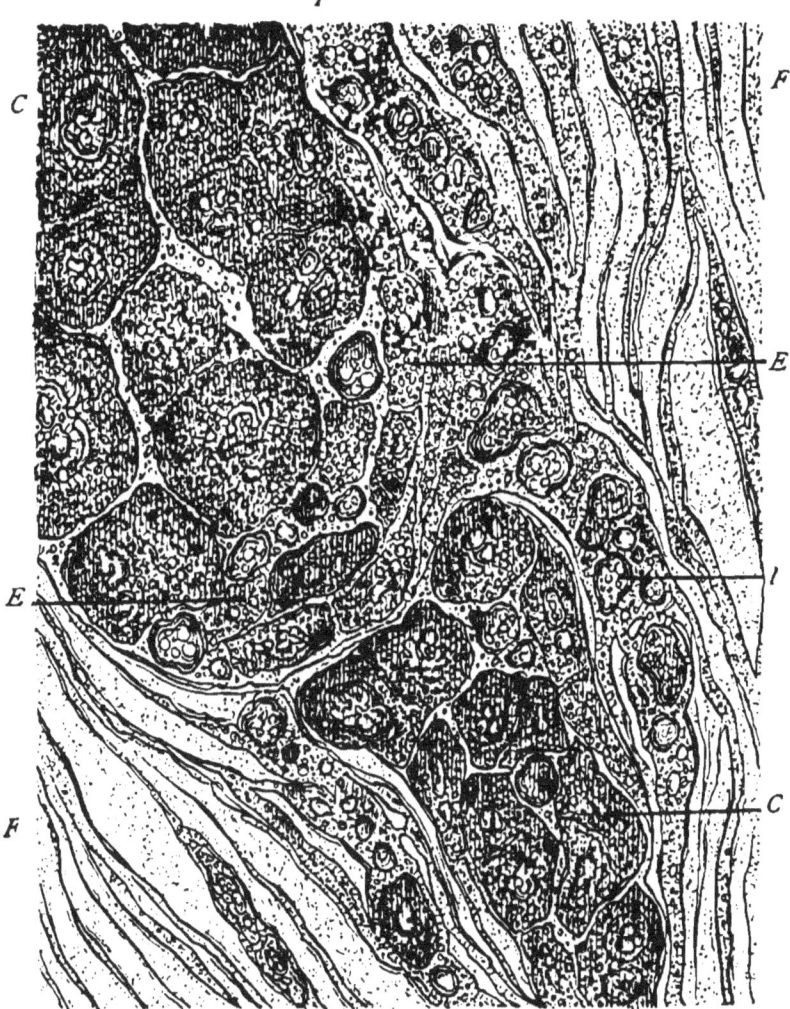

FIG. 6.—Tissue Changes around a Lymph-Vessel filled with Cancer Epithelia. × 1,000. *F, F*, fibrous connective tissue unchanged ; *C, C*, cancer epithelia in a lymph-vessel, coarsely granular, undergoing divisions ; *E, E*, endothelia lining the lymph-vessel in active proliferation ; *I, I*, proliferation of fibrous connective tissue environing the cancer thrombus.

stance of the fibrous connective tissue has, to a large extent, been liquefied and transformed into protoplasm, so much so that only scanty spindle-shaped vestiges of such tissue are seen in the immediate vicinity of the lymph-vessels; whereas, some distance away, the beginning liquefaction of the basis substance is shown by the reappearance of living matter. The peritoneal cover of the left tube is broadened, its blood-vessels dilated, and the cortex crowded with medullary or inflammatory corpuscles. In a few places I was able to trace an increase in the size of the medullary corpuscles to that of cancer epithelia, so much so that I must attribute the inflammatory infiltration of the peritoneum not to peritonitis proper, but to a beginning invasion of the peritoneum with cancer.

My researches prove, beyond doubt, that the spreading of cancer from one organ, or from one tissue toward a neighboring one, is accomplished by the lymph-vessels—immaterial whether in a centrifugal or centripetal direction. For centuries physicians and pathologists have been aware of the fact that the organs first affected by secondary cancerous growth are the lymph-ganglia in the neighborhood. It was a logical inference to conclude that the lymphatics were instrumental in conveying the poison of the cancer. It remained unsettled up to date whether the infection of the lymph ganglia was affected by the so-called cancer-juice or by constitutent elements of the cancerous growth.

No observation, as far as I am aware, has ever been made to corroborate the hypothesis of the pathologist. My studies have revealed the fact that the lymph vessels carry the cancer poison not only to the neighboring lymph ganglia, therefore, centrifugally, but into an organ which has no lymph ganglia, only lymph-vessels, as the ovary. The specimen shows plainly that the poison is the cancer epithelia which are transmitted into the lymphatics, causing thrombosis of the lymphatics and infection around them. Whether or not the poison is lodged in parasitic organisms within the cancer epithelia I am unable to say.

All attempts to prove the existence of such parasites have thus far proven to be a failure.

Professor Dr. P. Foa, in his article, "Ueber die Krebsparasiten,"[1] depicts star-shaped figures as parasitic organisms. These star-shaped figures are the reticulum in the protoplasm, described by Dr. C. Heitzman twenty years ago. Dr. J. Sawtscenko, in "Weitere Untersuchungen über schmarotzende Sporozoen, in den Krebsgeschwülsten," represents the same as micro-organisms.

Sir James Paget says: " I believe that micro-parasites, or substances produced by them, will some day be found in essential relation with cancers and cancerous diseases."[2]

F. A. Purcell remarks:[3] " Cancer-cells show amoeboid movements, and can thus travel independently in tissue spaces, or even penetrate delicate membranes, so that the cancer germs may thus travel by their own power, or be carried along in the vascular systems or connective-tissue spaces in every possible direction."

But as yet none of these suppositions have been demonstrated. John Marshall, F.R.S., speaks of " the acid juices of cancer, and the mode in which they penetrate into the vacuities of living tissue;" adding, " the elements must pass into the intervals between the surrounding tissue, they must go into the lymphatics, they must reach the lymphatic glands. The proof of this is that the lymphatic glands in the neighborhood are always the first to be infected."[4]

Reed, of Cincinnati, observes: " The disease must advance either by the continuous invasion of adjacent normal tissue or by migration of cell elements either through the lymphatics or hemic circulations."

Virchow says: " I have come to the conclusion, the only one I think the facts warrant, that the infection is directly transferred by the means of the morbid juices from the original seat of the disease to the anastomosing ele-

[1] Centralblatt für Bakteriologie und Parasitenkunde. Band xii., 1892.
[2] Morton Lecture, 1887.
[3] Purcell on Cancer.
[4] Morton Lecture, 1889.

ments in the neighborhood without the intervention of the vessels and nerves. The nerves are, indeed, often the best conductors for the propagation of contagious new formations, not as nerves, but as parts with soft interstitial tissue. An ichorous juice may pass from a cancerous tumor through the lungs without producing any change in them, and get at a very remote point, as for example in the liver, or a very distant part, and excite change of a malignant nature." [1]

Dr. George F. Shrady's statement, in his above-mentioned article, is nearer the truth, is, indeed, the exact fact. He says: "We know the cells are the cause of infection. Cancer progresses by a transport of its proliferating cells into neighboring parts." [2]

Another late authority, G. Sims Woodhead, says: "I shall not attempt to enter into any discussion as to the relative frequency of the spread of cancer by blood-vessels and by lymphatics, although lately some doubt has been thrown on the accuracy of our present teaching in regard to this question. I will merely state that I am more and more convinced that cancer exists almost entirely in the lymphatic vessel." [3]

Recklinghausen, in his article "Ueber die venöse Embolie und den retrograden Transport in den Venen und in den Lymphgefässen," observes: "Our attention was called to the circumstance that white cords of the thickness of a feather were on the surface of the right lung, which cords, on account of their form and arrangements, could not be anything else than thickened subpleural lymphatic vessels filled with sarcoma mass." [4]

We notice Recklinghausen simply infers this. In all the authorities I have been able to consult I find it nowhere stated that the lymphatics have been seen carrying the cancer epithelia, and forming in distant spots centres of infection or new cancer nests.

[1] Cellular Pathology. [2] MEDICAL RECORD, 1887.
[3] British Medical Journal, May 7, 1892.
[4] Virchow: Archiv. vol. c.

www.ingramcontent.com/pod-product-compliance
Lightning Source LLC
Chambersburg PA
CBHW022001100426
42738CB00042B/1366